NEARNESS

A Journey into Intimacy with God

Oluwakemi T. Amuda

Copyright Page

This book is a work of personal reflection and spiritual exploration. Unless otherwise indicated, all Scripture quotations are taken from the Holy Bible.

Published by Kemi A. Global Press

Printed in the United States of America

Dedication

This book is dedicated to the One who first drew near.

To God, who longed for a relationship with me long before I understood what intimacy meant. To the Holy Spirit, my Teacher and Companion, who patiently led me into a deeper walk with God. And to Jesus Christ, who made a way for me to come close without fear.

May every page reflect His heart, His gentleness, His patience, and His invitation to come nearer.

To those who are hungry.
To those who are tired of surface-level faith.
To those who whisper their prayers and wonder whether God is listening. May this book not only speak to you but also lead you into His presence.

Preface

This book was not written because I have mastered intimacy with God. It was written because I am learning it. I am learning what it means to slow down, to listen, to be still, and to truly know Him, not just through words but through relationship.

There were moments while writing this book when God gently showed me where my heart was distant, distracted, or divided. In those moments, this book became more than something I was writing; it became something God was using to shape me.

This is not a book of conclusions. It is a journey. My prayer is simple: that as you read, you will not just gain understanding but begin to experience God differently. That your desire for Him will deepen. And that you will discover that intimacy with God is not reserved for a few; it is available to you.

Author's Note

I did not approach this book as someone who has reached a place of nearness to God. I approached it as someone still learning to walk with God.

Intimacy is not something you achieve; it is something you grow into. And I am still growing.

This book does not contain formulas. You will not find swift solutions. Instead, what is offered here is an invitation: an invitation to slow down, to draw closer, and to allow God to meet you personally.

If at any moment during your reading you sense that God is drawing your heart, please pause. Do not hurry past this moment. The purpose of this book is not the acquisition of knowledge itself; rather, it is to know Him.

Table of Contents

Introduction

There is more to prayer than merely requesting. There is a realm where prayer takes on a more profound quality, quieter, more genuine, and more authentic. It is a place where one no longer merely addresses God but becomes increasingly aware of His presence. A place where the heart begins to harmonise with His.

This is what is called intimacy.

Many believers know how to pray; however, few have mastered the art of communion with God. Without intimacy, prayer risks becoming perfunctory, laden with words yet devoid of meaningful connection.

This publication is an invitation to a deeper experience. Not to pray more, but to draw nearer. For when one approaches God more closely, prayer transforms.

It shifts from being predominantly about asking to being primarily about understanding. From exertion to relationship. From striving to reach God to recognising His constant nearness.

This constitutes a journey into that form of relationship. As you engage with this text, do not rush.

Take your time.

Pause when necessary.

Allow God to communicate.

The objective of this publication is to have you initiate a walk with God unlike any you've had before.

PART I

FOUNDATIONS OF DISTANCE AND RETURN

CHAPTER ONE

Drawing Near to God

The Beginning of the Journey

There comes a moment in the life of a believer when prayer begins to feel deeper than words. At first, prayer is simple. We learn to speak to God. We learn to bring our needs before Him. We learn to ask, request, and express what is in our hearts. In many ways, this is where the journey begins.

Over time, something shifts within us. Prayer begins to raise questions we did not expect. We begin to wonder why we can speak to God and still feel distant. Why can we pray and still feel as if something is missing?

Why are the words there, but the sense of closeness is not always present?

These questions are not signs of spiritual failure. They are often the beginning of something deeper. They are the beginning of hunger. And hunger is where intimacy begins to grow. Because prayer was never meant to remain only as speaking, it was meant to bring one closer to God.

God Has Always Been the One Drawing Near

Before man ever reached for God, God was already reaching for man. In the garden, after Adam and Eve had sinned, we see God walking and calling, "Where are you?" (Genesis 3:9). That question was not because God lacked information. It was because the relationship had been broken and distance had entered where closeness once existed.

From that moment, the story of Scripture becomes the story of God pursuing man back into relationship, not merely into obedience or religion, but into fellowship.

This pursuit recurs in the words of Jesus, who says, "Come to Me, all who are weary and burdened" (Matthew 11:28). The invitation is not to a system or a practice, but to Himself.

God has always initiated closeness. He is not distant; he is waiting to be found. He is near, inviting the heart to respond. The real question is no longer whether God desires closeness, but whether we recognise and respond to His invitation.

When Prayer Becomes Familiar but Not Close

It is possible to pray regularly and still feel distant from God. Many believers know this experience in silence. They pray, but their hearts sometimes feel far from what their lips are saying. They speak, but do not always sense a connection. They go through familiar rhythms of prayer, yet something within still longs for more.

This is not because God is absent. It is often because awareness of Him has grown weak. Jesus addressed this when He said, "These people honour Me with their lips, but their hearts are far from Me" (Matthew 15:8). The issue was not the presence of words. It was the absence of closeness.

Distance from God does not always happen suddenly. It often happens slowly, through distraction, busyness, routine, and the pressures of life. Without realising it, prayer can become something we do rather than a place where we meet God.

What It Means to Draw Near

Drawing near to God is not about trying harder. It is about learning to be with Him. It is the simple yet profound shift from merely speaking to God to becoming aware of Him in prayer.

It is learning that He is not only the One we talk to, but the One we are with. James writes, "Draw near to God, and He will draw near to you" (James 4:8). This is not merely instruction; it is relationship. As the heart turns towards God, awareness of His nearness grows. This nearness is not always emotional or dramatic. Sometimes it is quiet. Sometimes it is steady. Sometimes it is a gentle awareness that God is present even when nothing feels extraordinary.

Over time, this awareness begins to shape everything else in the believer's life.

How Intimacy Begins to Form

Intimacy with God does not begin as a finished experience. It begins as a growing relationship. It begins when a person starts to slow down in God's presence.

When prayer is no longer only about requests but about staying with Him.

When silence becomes part of the relationship, not something to avoid.

As this grows, something begins to shift within the heart. Desires begin to change. Priorities begin to realign. The inner life begins to soften and adjust. David described this kind of relationship when he said, "My soul thirsts after You" (Psalm 63:8). That language speaks of pursuit and closeness. It is not distant admiration. It is an active relationship. Intimacy grows quietly yet deeply, not through pressure but through time; not through performance but through presence.

When Prayer Begins to Change

As closeness with God increases, prayer naturally begins to transform. You begin to pray differently, not because you learned new techniques, but because your heart is changing. You become more aware of God as you pray. You begin to speak honestly. You begin to listen more carefully. You begin to sense that prayer is not only about what you say, but about who you are with.

Jesus describes this kind of life when He says, "Abide in Me, and I in you" (John 15:4). Abiding is not an activity; it is a way of remaining. It means staying close enough for the relationship to be continuous, not occasional. From this place, prayer is no longer just a moment in the day. It becomes a way of living with God.

The Invitation into Closeness

This is where the journey truly begins. Not with correction. Not with pressure. But with an invitation. An invitation to return to closeness with God. To slow down within. To become aware again.

To allow the heart to turn towards Him, even in small ways, because God is not far from you. He is not waiting at a distance, unwilling to be known. He is near. He is present. He is already reaching towards the heart.

The journey of intimacy begins when the heart responds. Even in weakness. Even in uncertainty. Even in small steps. Because God responds to those who seek Him sincerely. “You will seek Me and find Me when you seek Me with all your heart” (Jeremiah 29:13).

The Foundation of Everything Else

Everything that follows in this book rests on this truth: before prayer becomes powerful, it must become personal. And before it becomes personal, the heart must learn to draw near. This is the foundation of intimacy with God. Not distance. Not performance. Not routine.

But closeness. As this journey continues, we will see how intimacy reshapes prayer, transforms desire, and forms the believer's inner life. Yet everything begins here, with a simple turning of the heart towards God.

CHAPTER TWO

When Prayer Becomes Familiar but Distant

There is a kind of spiritual experience many believers go through, but do not always know how to describe. It is neither a falling away from God nor a rejection of faith. On the surface, everything still looks intact. Prayer continues. Church life continues. Scripture is still read. Spiritual language is still spoken.

Yet inside, something begins to feel different.

There is activity, but less awareness. There is prayer, but less sense of encounter. There is faith, but sometimes less felt nearness. This is one of the quietest places a believer can find themselves, not because God has moved away, but because the heart has slowly adjusted to distance without realising it.

Scripture gives language to this experience when Jesus says, “These people honour Me with their lips, but their hearts are far from Me” (Matthew 15:8). The issue is not the absence of words. It is the distance of the heart. Expression can remain even as awareness weakens within.

This is how spiritual life becomes familiar, yet not always close.

Familiarity is not inherently negative. It often comes through repeated exposure to spiritual life. We learn to pray, to speak in Christian settings, to respond in worship, and to navigate Scripture. But when familiarity is not guarded by intentional awareness, it slowly diminishes hunger. And when hunger diminishes, pursuit becomes lighter. When pursuit becomes lighter, awareness becomes less sharp.

And this is where the quiet drift begins.

It rarely announces itself. It does not come through rebellion. It comes through life, through responsibilities, thoughts, emotions, and daily pressures that gradually capture attention. The heart does not reject God; it simply becomes divided.

This is why Scripture says, "Unite my heart to fear Your name" (Psalm 86:11). The psalmist understood that the heart can scatter. It can remain religious in expression while divided in affection. When the heart is divided, prayer remains, but depth begins to thin.

It is important to understand that God does not move in this process. He does not withdraw His presence from His people. Scripture is consistent: "The Lord is near to all who call on Him" (Psalm 145:18).

Nearness is not the issue.

Awareness is.

The real struggle is not whether God is present, but whether the heart is attentive to what is already true. This is why Jesus says, "Abide in Me, and I in you" (John 15:4). Abiding is not occasional contact. It is a sustained awareness of the relationship. The branch does not survive through periodic contact with the vine; it survives by remaining in it. In the same way, the believer is not meant to visit God only in prayer, but to remain aware of Him throughout life.

Yet life naturally pulls attention outward. Responsibilities increase. Thoughts multiply. Concerns weigh on the mind. Without intentional return, inward awareness begins to fade, not because God is absent, but because attention has shifted.

This is why Scripture calls the believer back to stillness: "Be still, and know that I am God" (Psalm 46:10). Stillness is not inactivity. It is the return of attention.

It is the quieting of internal noise so that what is already true is recognised again. Yet stillness is often the first thing lost in a busy life. Without stillness, prayer can feel like movement without depth, words spoken without inner alignment, and thoughts expressed without inner awareness.

At this stage, many believers do not stop praying. They simply notice that prayer feels different from what it used to be. There is still consistency, but less sensitivity. Still structured, but fewer encounters. Still believe, but less awareness of nearness.

This is not a condemnation. It is recognition.

God does not reject a believer in this place. He calls them back to awareness. "Return to Me, and I will return to you," says the Lord of hosts (Malachi 3:7). Return is not about reacceptance; it is about restored attentiveness.

One danger of this condition is that it can feel normal. And what feels normal is often the hardest to notice. A believer can function spiritually while slowly losing depth of communion. They still pray, still serve, still believe, but something within quietly longs for more than routine expression.

David expresses this longing when he says, "As the deer pants for streams of water, so my soul pants for You, O God" (Psalm 42:1–2). This is not an obligation. It is a desire. It is the recognition that something essential is missing when closeness is diminished. And that longing is not a problem. It is a signal.

It is the heart remembering its design.

Human life with God was never meant to function at a distance. It was designed for closeness, awareness, communion, and fellowship, where God is not only believed in but consciously known.

This is why Jesus consistently addresses the heart, not only behaviour but also inward alignment. The danger is not only outward disobedience but also the unnoticed inward distance. When the believer begins to see this clearly, something important shifts. Awareness awakens again. And awareness is always the beginning of restoration.

Because intimacy does not begin with intensity. It begins with recognition.

Recognition that prayer has become familiar but less alive. Recognition that awareness of God has weakened. Recognition that closeness is no longer what it used to feel like. And in that recognition, God is not offended. He invites. He calls the heart back—not into pressure, but into relationship. Not into performance, but into nearness. Not into striving, but into awareness.

This is why Scripture says, "Draw near to God, and He will draw near to you" (James 4:8).

The movement is relational. The invitation is mutual. The response is closeness.

This chapter is not a rebuke. It is a mirror.

It does not say the believer has lost God. It reveals that the heart may have lost awareness of how near He still is. Once that is clearly seen, something begins to shift inwardly.

The journey back to intimacy does not begin with effort.

It begins with awareness.

And awareness begins with honesty before God.

CHAPTER THREE

The Quiet Crisis of The Heart

There is a kind of struggle in the life of a believer that does not always announce itself loudly. It does not always appear as open rebellion or a visible departure from faith. In fact, it often exists within lives that still appear steady in their walk with God. Prayer is still practised. Scripture is still read.

Church life is still maintained. Words about God are still spoken with sincerity.

And yet, beneath all of this outward consistency, something can begin to shift quietly within the heart. It is not always easy to describe. It is not always easy to admit. But there is a difference between being spiritually active and being spiritually aware.

There is a difference between continuing religious practice and living in deep, conscious fellowship with God. Over time, a believer may find themselves functioning in faith while sensing less closeness than before.

This is what can be described as the quiet crisis of the heart.

It is quiet because it rarely begins with a dramatic change. It develops slowly through ordinary life, through distractions that seem harmless, through legitimate but consuming responsibilities, through necessary but constant thoughts, and through emotional and mental preoccupations that gradually erode inward stillness.

Without realising it, the heart begins to carry more than it was meant to carry at once. And in carrying too much, it begins to lose the simplicity of awareness of God.

Scripture gives language to this condition when it says, “Keep your heart with all diligence, for out of it spring the issues of life” (Proverbs 4:23). The heart is not passive. It is shaped by what it repeatedly attends to, what it values, and what it returns to in thought and affection. When attention becomes divided, the heart gradually becomes divided as well.

This is why the psalmist prays, “Unite my heart to fear Your name” (Psalm 86:11). That prayer is not merely poetic. It recognises that the heart can become fragmented, pulled in different directions, carrying competing desires, and overwhelmed by life’s pressures. When the heart is not united, spiritual life does not cease, but it loses depth.

This is how a believer can still pray while feeling less inward connection, still worship while feeling less aware, and still believe while sensing less nearness. Not because God has changed, but because attention has shifted.

One of the most important truths at this stage is that God does not withdraw from His people in moments like this. Scripture consistently reveals a God who remains near: "The Lord is near to all who call upon Him" (Psalm 145:18). His nearness is not dependent on emotional awareness. It is rooted in His nature. He is not distant by default and present only occasionally; He is present by nature and remains near even when the heart is not fully aware of Him.

The struggle, then, is not the absence of God, but a reduced awareness of Him.

This is where many believers begin to experience something they cannot always define. Prayer continues, but it feels less alive. Scripture is read, but it feels less engaging. Worship is offered, but it feels less internally connected. The structure remains, but the sense of encounter feels less consistent.

This does not mean God is absent in those moments. It means awareness is not fully present with Him. Awareness can fade quietly when life becomes crowded. Jesus speaks to this reality when He says, “The cares of this world and the deceitfulness of riches choke the word” (Matthew 13:22). The word “choke” describes gradual restriction rather than sudden removal, something that slowly grows over what once had life, reducing its expression over time.

This is how distraction works in the heart. It rarely removes God from life. It reduces the conscious space in which God is recognised. The heart remains active, but less attentive. Faith remains, though awareness weakens. Prayer remains, though depth becomes less consistent.

Over time, a believer can become familiar with the things of God without remaining equally conscious of God Himself. This is one of the most subtle shifts in spiritual life.

Familiarity with language, routines, and environments can remain strong even as inward sensitivity quietly weakens. This is what Jesus addresses when He says, “These people honour Me with their lips, but their hearts are far from Me” (Matthew 15:8). The issue is not a lack of expression but a distance of heart. It is possible to continue speaking about God while gradually losing the inward depth of connection with Him.

This is why this stage is not about condemnation but about recognition. What is not recognised cannot be restored. And what is mistaken for normal cannot be addressed intentionally.

The believer at this stage is not necessarily far from God in reality, but may be far in awareness. There is a difference between position and perception. In position, God remains near. In perception, the heart may not always clearly recognise that nearness.

This is why Scripture calls believers back to awareness rather than to relocation: "Be still, and know that I am God" (Psalm 46:10). Stillness is not merely the absence of activity; it is the return of attention. It is the quieting of inner noise so that what is already true can be recognised again.

When life becomes filled with constant mental, emotional, and practical engagement, stillness becomes less frequent. Without stillness, awareness of God becomes less sharp, even as faith remains intact.

At this point, many believers continue faithfully in their spiritual life but begin to notice a quiet longing for something deeper. A sense that prayer could be more than it currently feels. A sense that the relationship with God could be more conscious, more alive, and more present in daily awareness. This longing is important because it is not loss, it is often an awakening.

Scripture describes this longing when it says, "As the deer pants for streams of water, so my soul pants for You, O God" (Psalm 42:1–2). This is not a casual desire. It is a deep inward thirst. It is the heart remembering its purpose.

That longing is not to be ignored. It is not a problem to be silenced. It is often the beginning of a return.

Even in the quiet crisis of the heart, God has not withdrawn His invitation. He remains near, calling the heart back to awareness. "Return to Me, and I will return to you," says the Lord (Malachi 3:7).

Return is not God becoming present again; it is the heart becoming aware again. And this is where hope begins to emerge. The quiet crisis is not the end of intimacy. It is often the moment when intimacy is desired again, with honesty.

The believer begins to recognise, sometimes slowly, sometimes clearly, that prayer was never meant to be merely an activity. It was meant to be an awareness of God. It was meant to be a relationship. It was meant to be closeness.

And once that recognition takes hold, the journey begins to turn again.

Not into pressure.

Not into performance.

But in return.

Return to awareness.

Return to simplicity.

Return to God.

Because the crisis was never that God moved away. The crisis was that the heart began to notice Him less. And once that is seen clearly, the path forward is no longer one of confusion.

CHAPTER FOUR

God Has Not Moved

There is a moment in the journey of faith when a believer begins to question what has changed in their relationship with God. It is not always spoken aloud, nor is it always fully understood. Yet inwardly, there can be a growing sense that something feels different.

Prayer may still be present, but it sometimes feels less engaging. Worship may still be practised, but it sometimes feels less expressive. Scripture may still be read, but it sometimes feels less alive in the moment of reading. In that quiet space, a question begins to form in the heart: Has something changed between God and me?

This question is important because the answer shapes the direction of spiritual life.

One truth must be established early and firmly: God has not moved. Scripture consistently reveals a God who remains steadfast in His nearness to His people. “The Lord is near to all who call upon Him” (Psalm 145:18). Not occasionally near. Not selectively near. Near to all who call upon Him. His nearness is not dependent on human awareness. It is grounded in His unchanging nature.

This means that when a believer feels distant, the first conclusion must not be that God has withdrawn. The foundation of truth does not allow that interpretation. God does not shift His presence towards His people in response to fluctuating human experience. He remains faithful, steady, and near.

This is why Scripture also says, “I am the Lord, I do not change” (Malachi 3:6). God's consistency is not emotional. It is eternal. He does not become more or less present on certain days.

He does not move closer when the believer feels strong, nor does He move farther when the believer feels weak. His nearness remains constant.

The struggle, then, is not the movement of God. It is the awareness of man.

There is a difference between reality and recognition. God can be fully present even when the heart is only partially aware. This gap between presence and awareness is where many tensions in spiritual life are felt.

This is why Scripture calls the believer to awareness rather than relocation: "Be still, and know that I am God" (Psalm 46:10). Stillness is not about drawing God closer. It is about becoming aware of what is already true. It is the quieting of inner noise so that reality can be recognised again.

When life becomes filled with activity, thought, responsibility, and emotional weight, stillness becomes rare.

And when stillness becomes rare, awareness becomes less consistent, not because God is absent, but because attention is divided. This is one of the most important realities in spiritual life: attention shapes awareness. What the heart consistently attends to becomes what it is most aware of.

This is why Scripture calls believers to guard the heart. “Keep your heart with all diligence, for out of it spring the issues of life” (Proverbs 4:23). The heart is not passive. It is continually shaped by what it repeatedly focuses on.

When attention is drawn to worries, responsibilities, or internal noise, awareness of God does not disappear, but it becomes less sharp. The believer still believes in God, prays, and acknowledges Him, yet the sense of nearness feels less immediate than before.

This is where misunderstanding can begin if the truth is not firmly established.

In moments of diminished awareness, the human heart can mistake experience for truth. A believer may feel distant and, over time, come to accept that feeling as reality. But Scripture does not allow feeling to define truth. Truth defines experience, not the other way around.

God is near, even when He is not strongly felt. God is present, even when awareness is weak. God is faithful, even when perception fluctuates.

This is why faith is essential to the Christian life. Faith is not a denial of experience; it is an alignment with truth beyond experience. It is the decision to trust what God has said, even when emotions are not fully aligned in the moment. Hebrews describes faith as "the substance of things hoped for, the evidence of things not seen" (Hebrews 11:1). Faith becomes the bridge between divine reality and human awareness.

It holds firm when feelings shift.

When a believer feels distant, the right response is not panic or assumption. The right response is to return to the truth.

And truth says: God has not moved.

This truth protects the heart from unnecessary discouragement. Many believers interpret spiritual dryness as a sign of divine absence. But dryness is not distance. A lack of feeling is not a lack of presence. Silence is not absence.

God remains present in silence.

God remains present in dryness.

God remains present in moments when awareness feels weak.

This is why Scripture calls believers to return, not because God has moved away, but because attention has drifted. "Return to Me, and I will return to you," says the Lord (Malachi 3:7).

This is not about relocation. It is about relational restoration.

Return is about restoring awareness, not reestablishing presence. In the life of prayer, this distinction is essential. If a believer believes God has moved away, prayer becomes a striving to reach Him again. But if a believer understands that God is already near, prayer becomes the process of returning awareness.

This changes everything about prayer.

Instead of trying to reach a distant God, the heart begins to quiet itself to recognise a present God. Instead of trying to gain God's attention, the believer learns to remove distractions so awareness can be restored. This is where intimacy begins to deepen again.

Intimacy is not built by closing the distance through effort. It is deepened by recognising nearness through awareness. Jesus expresses this truth in deeply relational language when He says, "Abide in Me, and I in you" (John 15:4).

Abiding is not movement towards a distant place. It is remaining in a present relationship. It is a continuous awareness of connection. It is living in conscious union. The branch does not search for the vine. It remains in the vine. The challenge is not the connection itself, but awareness of it.

In the same way, the believer is not called to find a faraway God. The believer is invited to remain aware of being near God.

This is why spiritual life is often a journey of returning attention rather than achieving distance or closure. The heart is trained, again and again, to return to awareness of God, in prayer, in Scripture, in silence, and in daily life.

And over time, something begins to shift.

The believer begins to notice God again in places where they once felt nothing. Prayer begins to feel less like effort and more like awareness.

Scripture begins to feel less like reading and more like an encounter. Worship begins to feel less like expression alone and more like a response. Not because God has changed, but because awareness has been restored.

This is the gentle work of God in intimacy. He does not withdraw and demand pursuit from a distance. He remains near and invites awareness to return. This is why Scripture says, “Draw near to God, and He will draw near to you” (James 4:8). The movement is not spatial. It is relational awareness becoming clearer. As the heart turns towards Him, nearness is experienced more consciously.

This chapter is therefore not about correcting a distant God. It is about correcting a mistaken perception. God has not changed position. The heart is invited to see clearly again. And this is where confusion begins to turn into clarity.

Once a believer truly understands that God has not moved, they no longer try to find Him at a distance.

They learn to recognise Him in nearness.

And that recognition is where intimacy begins to deepen again.

CHAPTER FIVE

Prayer Was Never Meant to Be Transactional

There is a way many believers learn to pray that feels natural at first, because it is rooted in real human need. When life becomes heavy, when uncertainty rises, when questions multiply, the instinct is to speak to God about what is happening. To ask Him for help. To present needs. To seek intervention.

God is gracious in this. He hears. He responds. He cares deeply about His children's concerns. Scripture is clear: "Call upon Me in the day of trouble; I will deliver you" (Psalm 50:15). God does not reject the cries of His people. But over time, something subtle can begin to form in the way prayer is understood.

Without realising it, prayer can slowly shift from relationship into request, from communion into exchange, from closeness into transaction.

This shift is rarely intentional. It happens quietly, through repeated need-based prayer without deeper awareness of God Himself. A believer begins to associate prayer primarily with asking and receiving, needing and solutions, problems and answers.

While God does respond to needs, prayer was never meant to remain at the level of transaction.

At its core, prayer is not a system of exchange. It is a relationship of communion. Jesus reveals this distinction when He teaches His disciples to pray. He begins not with requests but with a relationship: "Our Father in heaven" (Matthew 6:9). Before any petition is made, identity is established. Before any need is expressed, the relationship is acknowledged.

This matters deeply.

If prayer begins with need alone, it can easily become centred on the self. But if prayer begins with relationship, it becomes centred on God. The difference between these foundations shapes the entire life of prayer.

When prayer becomes primarily transactional, the focus gradually shifts towards outcomes, what is needed, what is lacking, what must change, what must be provided. While none of these are wrong to bring before God, they are not meant to be the foundation of connection with Him.

Over time, this kind of prayer can begin to feel like a cycle of asking and waiting, asking and hoping, asking and receiving. And when answers are delayed or do not come as expected, discouragement can quietly enter the heart. Not because God is unfaithful, but because the foundation of the relationship has been reduced to exchange.

This is why Scripture gently reorders the heart when it says, “Seek first the kingdom of God and His righteousness, and all these things shall be added to you” (Matthew 6:33). The order is important. Relationship comes first. Provision follows. Seeking God comes first. Added things follow.

God is not opposed to providing, but He is committed to something deeper than provision. He is committed to relationship. This is why Jesus also says, “Your Father knows what you need before you ask Him” (Matthew 6:8). This shifts prayer from informing God to encountering God.

If God already knows what is needed, prayer is not about updating Him. It is about drawing near to Him.

This changes the posture of prayer entirely.

Prayer is no longer only about what is spoken, but about what is formed within the heart in His presence.

Many believers unknowingly carry a transactional mindset into their prayer life. They approach God primarily as the One who solves problems. While He is indeed a Helper, He is also a Father. The difference between a Helper and a Father is the relationship.

A Helper responds to requests. A Father responds to a relationship.

This is why Jesus consistently uses the word "Father" when teaching about prayer. He is not introducing terminology; He is revealing identity. God is not distant, responding only to demands. He is near, responding to sons and daughters who know Him.

This is why Scripture says, "As many as are led by the Spirit of God, these are sons of God"

(Romans 8:14). Sonship is relational before it is functional. It is being with God before it is receiving from God.

When prayer becomes transactional, something subtle begins to happen within the believer. God can gradually be associated primarily with provision rather than presence, with answers rather than relationship, with help rather than communion. And when that happens, prayer can remain active, but intimacy begins to weaken, because intimacy cannot grow in a purely transactional environment. It requires presence, awareness, and relationship.

This is why Scripture continually calls believers back to closeness: "Draw near to God, and He will draw near to you" (James 4:8). Drawing near is relational language. It is not exchanging language. It is a connection language. God is not inviting His people into a system where requests are processed. He is inviting them into a relationship where He is known.

This is where the heart begins to be reshaped.

When a believer begins to see prayer as a relationship rather than a transaction, their approach to God changes.

They still bring needs, but not only needs.
They still ask, but not only ask.
They begin to stay.
They begin to listen.
They begin to become aware.

Prayer begins to shift from a place of request alone to a place of encounter.

This is what Jesus demonstrates when He says, "Abide in Me, and I in you" (John 15:4). Abiding is not transactional. It is relational continuity. It is remaining, not visiting. It is a connection, not an exchange.

A branch does not relate to the vine through requests. It relates through connection. Life flows because a connection exists, not because negotiation takes place. In the same way, the believer is not meant to relate to God primarily through need, but through union.

This does not remove asking from prayer. It reorders it. Needs are still expressed, but they are no longer the centre. Relationship becomes the centre. And when the relationship becomes the centre, something shifts internally.

Prayer becomes less anxious. It becomes less pressured. It becomes less performance-driven because the believer is no longer trying to secure God's response. They are resting in God's presence.

This is why Scripture says, "Be anxious for nothing, but in everything by prayer and supplication… let your requests be made known to God" (Philippians 4:6).

Requests are not removed; they are placed within peace, not pressure, within relationship, not anxiety. The result is not only answers but peace: “And the peace of God, which surpasses all understanding, will guard your hearts and minds through Christ Jesus” (Philippians 4:7).

Notice what is guarded: the heart and the mind. Transactional prayer often produces internal instability when outcomes are uncertain. By contrast, relational prayer produces stability even in waiting, because the foundation is not in outcomes, but in God Himself.

This is the shift in intimacy that prayer brings.

It does not remove desire. It purifies it.
It does not remove asking. It deepens the relationship.
It does not reduce prayer. It transforms. Requests are not removed; they are placed within peace, not pressure, within relationship, not anxiety.

The result is not only answers but peace: “And the peace of God, which surpasses all understanding, will guard your hearts and minds through Christ Jesus” (Philippians 4:7). Notice what is guarded: the heart and the mind. Transactional prayer often breeds internal instability when outcomes are uncertain. By contrast, relational prayer fosters stability even in waiting, because the foundation is not in outcomes, but in God Himself.

This is the shift in intimacy that prayer brings.

It does not remove desire. It purifies it. It does not remove asking. It deepens the relationship.
It does not reduce prayer. It transforms it. it.

The believer begins to understand that the grcatcst gift of prayer is not only what comes from God’s hand, but God Himself.

And when that becomes clear, prayer is no longer measured only by what is received. It is also measured by how close the heart has become.

This is the heart of intimacy.

Not a system of exchange.
But a life of relationships.

And once this truth settles in the heart, prayer can never be the same again.

Because the believer is no longer coming to God primarily for things.

They are coming to God for Him.

CHAPTER SIX

From Asking to Knowing

There is a moment in a believer's journey when something begins to shift quietly in the inner life of prayer. It is neither sudden nor dramatic. It rarely arrives with a clear announcement or an emotional breakthrough that can be easily explained to others. Instead, it develops slowly, almost unnoticed, through repeated encounters with God in prayer.

At the beginning of the journey, prayer is often shaped by need. The believer comes to God with requests, concerns, and burdens. There is nothing wrong with this. Scripture invites it. The psalmist says, "Cast your burden on the Lord, and He shall sustain you" (Psalm 55:22). God receives the honest weight of human life. He is not offended by dependence. In fact, He welcomes it.

So the believer learns to ask.

They ask for help in moments of weakness. They ask for direction when confused. They ask for provisions when lacking. They ask for intervention when situations feel beyond control. And over time, they begin to see that God responds, not always as expected, not always immediately, but always faithfully.

Yet something begins to happen beneath the surface of answered prayer that the attentive heart cannot ignore.

Even when needs are met, a deeper longing remains unsatisfied by outcomes alone. Even when situations improve, a quiet awareness persists that something more is being invited into a relationship with God. Even when prayers are answered, the heart still senses that it was made for more than answers.

This is where the turning begins—from asking to knowing.

Jesus gives language to this deeper reality when He says, “And this is eternal life, that they may know You, the only true God, and Jesus Christ whom You have sent” (John 17:3). Eternal life is not defined primarily as length of time or future destination. It is defined as a relationship. To know God.

Not to know about Him. Not to know His works only. But to know Him.

This is where prayer begins to reveal its deeper purpose.

Prayer was never only about receiving things from God. It was always about entering a relationship with God. At the beginning, this truth is not always obvious, because need feels more immediate than relationship. Human pressure tends to draw attention toward solutions. But God, in His wisdom, is not only forming outcomes—He is forming people.

This is why Jesus begins prayer not with a request, but with a relationship: "Our Father in heaven" (Matthew 6:9). Before anything is asked, something is established. Identity. Belonging. Relationship.

This order is not accidental. It is formative. Because when prayer begins with asking alone, the heart can slowly become centred on outcomes. But when prayer begins with relationship, everything flows from connection.

Over time, as the believer continues in prayer, something begins to change internally. Prayer begins to shift from being only a place of expression to becoming a place of awareness. Words are still spoken, but something deeper begins to form beneath the words.

There are moments where silence begins to carry more weight than speech. Not silence as emptiness, but silence as awareness.

The awareness that God is not far away waiting at a distance for words to reach Him, but near in the very moment of prayer itself.

This is where knowing begins to form.

Knowing God is not a single experience. It is not achieved solely through intensity. It is formed through time in a relationship. Through return. Through awareness. Through repeated turning of the heart toward Him in daily life.

Scripture gently guides the heart into this reality when it says, “Be still, and know that I am God” (Psalm 46:10). Stillness is not inactivity. It is attention settled. It is the heart becoming quiet enough to recognise what is already true. God is not becoming God in that moment. He already is. Stillness is where the heart begins to see clearly again.

At this stage, prayer begins to change in nature. It is no longer only driven by urgency.

It begins to carry awareness. Even when words are spoken, there is a deeper sense that God is near in the speaking itself. Jesus reinforces this shift when He says, "Your Father knows what you need before you ask Him" (Matthew 6:8). If God already knows, then prayer is no longer about informing Him. It becomes about encountering Him.

And once encountering becomes central, prayer changes.

It is no longer only about communication upward. It becomes awareness inwardly.

At first, this can feel unfamiliar. The believer may still be learning how to remain in silence without feeling like something is missing. Because much of spiritual life has been formed around speaking, responding, and expressing. But slowly, something deeper begins to emerge, the realisation that God is not only encountered in words, but also in awareness.

This is where the heart begins to shift from asking to knowing. Not by rejecting asking, but by moving beyond it as the center. As this continues, prayer becomes less anxious. Less pressured. Less driven by urgency alone. Because the believer begins to realise that they are not trying to reach a distant God, but relating to a present One.

This is where intimacy begins to deepen. Because intimacy is not sustained by requests alone. It is sustained by awareness of presence. David touches this when he says, “In Your presence is fullness of joy” (Psalm 16:11). Not in answers. Not in outcomes. In presence.

This changes what the believer begins to value most in prayer. Answers remain meaningful, but presence becomes central. Paul expresses this shift in desire when he says, “That I may know Him” (Philippians 3:10). Even after walking with God, even after ministry and revelation, the deepest longing remains unchanged: to know Him.

This reveals something essential. Spiritual maturity does not reduce desire; it refines it. It shifts desire from what God gives to God Himself. And as this shift deepens, prayer begins to stabilise internally. The believer is no longer only defined by whether prayers are answered quickly or visibly. They begin to recognise that even in waiting, they are with God. Even in silence, He is near. Even in delay, He is present.

This creates a deeper stability in the inner life. Because knowing God is no longer dependent on immediate outcomes, but on an ongoing relationship. Jesus describes this life simply: "Abide in Me, and I in you" (John 15:4). Abiding is a continuous relationship. Not occasional visits. Not isolated moments. Continuous awareness. A branch does not move in and out of the vine. It remains.

In the same way, the believer begins to understand that prayer is not only about coming to God but also about remaining aware of Him.

This is the shift from asking to knowing. Not a rejection of prayer requests, but a relocation of the centre.

And once this shift takes place, everything begins to change, not externally first, but inwardly. Because the believer is no longer coming to God primarily to get answers.

They are coming to know Him.

PART II

INNER LIFE OF INTIMACY

CHAPTER SEVEN

Learn to Listen to God

There is a stage in the life of a believer when prayer begins to mature beyond mere speech. At first, prayer is often filled with words. The believer comes before God with thoughts, needs, concerns, gratitude, and questions. There is comfort in speaking, because speech feels like a connection. It expresses what is inside and creates a sense of movement between the heart and God.

Over time, something begins to happen in the deeper life of a relationship with God. The believer starts to realise that prayer is not complete when only one side is speaking. Relationship, in its truest form, requires listening.

This realisation does not come as a theory. It comes through experience, through moments in prayer when words begin to slow down.

Through moments when the heart realises it has spoken much but has not paused to become aware of God Himself. Through moments when silence is no longer uncomfortable but meaningful. Scripture gently draws the believer into this reality: "Be still, and know that I am God" (Psalm 46:10).

Stillness is not emptiness. It is attention that has stopped scattering. It is the heart becoming quiet enough to recognise God not as a concept but as a present reality.

Listening to God does not begin with extraordinary experiences. It begins with attention. It begins with learning that a relationship is sustained not only by expression but also by awareness. Many believers struggle here because life trains them in speed, reaction, and constant mental activity.

Even prayer can become another form of movement, words filling space without the heart learning how to remain aware of God while speaking. Yet Scripture repeatedly draws the heart back to this place: “My soul, wait silently for God alone” (Psalm 62:5).

Waiting is not passivity. It is trust that refuses to rush ahead of awareness. It is the discipline of remaining before God without needing to fill every silence. In the spiritual life, listening is not primarily about hearing external sound. It is about becoming inwardly attentive to God’s presence and movement. It is the formation of a heart that can recognise God’s leading in quiet conviction, gentle correction, and inward clarity.

Jesus expresses this normality of relationship when He says, “My sheep hear My voice” (John 10:27). He does not describe hearing as rare. He describes it as belonging. Hearing God is part of a relationship, not a reward for spiritual achievement.

But this hearing is often quiet. It rarely competes with noise. It is recognised more for clarity than for volume, more for direction than for sound.

This is why listening requires inner stillness. A restless heart struggles to discern God. A distracted mind misreads conviction. A hurried life misses subtle guidance. Listening is not about God trying harder to speak. It is about the heart becoming still enough to recognise that He is already guiding.

This is why Elijah's experience matters deeply. In 1 Kings 19:11–12, wind, earthquake, and fire passed, but the Lord was not in them. Then came a gentle whisper. The point is not that God prefers silence to power. The point is that intimacy often requires sensitivity, not spectacle.

God is not absent in noise, but He is often recognised in quiet awareness. As the believer grows in this, prayer begins to change shape. It no longer feels like only speaking upwards. It begins to include moments of quiet awareness. The heart learns to pause, not out of obligation, but out of relationship.

Something begins to shift internally: urgency gives way to attentiveness; pressure gives way to awareness; striving gives way to trustful listening. Habakkuk captures this posture: “The Lord is in His holy temple; let all the earth keep silence before Him” (Habakkuk 2:20).

Silence here is reverence. It is recognition that God is not distant and waiting to be reached, but present and worthy of attention. As listening develops, clarity begins to grow in the believer’s life. Not because life becomes simpler, but because awareness becomes steadier. Confusion reduces not through more thinking, but through deeper alignment.

Proverbs explains this pattern: “In all your ways acknowledge Him, and He shall direct your paths” (Proverbs 3:6). Acknowledging God is not occasional. It is ongoing awareness.

It is the habit of bringing Him into the inward movement of life.

Over time, silence is no longer feared. It becomes a space of recognition. The believer begins to realise that God is encountered not only through words but also through awareness that grows in quietness. Jesus modelled this rhythm. He spoke, but He also withdrew to be with the Father (Luke 5:16). These moments were not a break from ministry; they were a deepening of awareness.

Listening also transforms obedience. It is no longer a blind effort to follow instructions. It becomes a relational response. The believer begins to follow God not only because of a command, but because of recognition. "My sheep hear My voice… and they follow Me" (John 10:27).

Hearing leads to following. Awareness leads to alignment. Relationship leads to movement. This is how intimacy deepens, not through more activity, but through deeper sensitivity. Prayer begins to include both speaking and listening, expression and awareness.

Request and stillness. Words and attention. And slowly, the believer realises something profound:

God was never far away.

They were learning how to recognise Him.

CHAPTER EIGHT

The Secret Place Is Not a Location

A phrase that has shaped the devotional imagination of many believers is "the secret place." It is often associated with silence, withdrawal, early mornings, closed doors, and physical separation from noise. These practices are helpful and even necessary for forming spiritual discipline. Jesus Himself said: "When you pray, go into your room, and shut the door" (Matthew 6:6).

But if the secret place is reduced to a physical environment, something essential is lost, because the secret place is not first a location.

It is a relational reality.

It is possible for a believer to enter a room, close the door, remove distractions, and still not enter the secret place inwardly.

It is also possible for a believer to be surrounded by noise, activity, and responsibility while remaining deeply aware of God. This is because the secret place is not defined by geography but by awareness of God. It is the place where the heart becomes conscious of Him.

David describes it this way: "He who dwells in the secret place of the Most High shall abide under the shadow of the Almighty" (Psalm 91:1). The language is not about visiting. It is about dwelling. Dwelling is continuity, not an occasion. It is not entering and leaving. It is remaining.

The secret place, therefore, is not where you go. It is where you live.

At the beginning of spiritual growth, believers often associate intimacy with external structure, quiet rooms, set times, and physical separation. These are valuable, but they are not the destination. They are training spaces for attention.

Because the deeper work of intimacy is not location change, but awareness formation.

Jesus clarifies this when He says: "Your Father who sees in secret will reward you openly" (Matthew 6:6). The emphasis is not on the secrecy of the environment, but on awareness of being seen by God. The secret place exists wherever the heart is aware of being before Him.

This means the believer can begin to experience the secret place in ordinary life, whether walking, working, waiting, or thinking, not because surroundings change, but because attention changes. Prayer, therefore, extends. It becomes an awareness carried through life. This is what Scripture points to when it says: "Pray without ceasing" (1 Thessalonians 5:17).

This is not constant speech. It is continuous awareness. A heart that returns again and again to God in the flow of life.

Jeremiah confirms this reality: "Do I not fill heaven and earth?" says the Lord (Jeremiah 23:24). If God fills all things, then the question is not His location, but our awareness. At the same time, Scripture affirms withdrawal. Jesus often withdrew to pray (Mark 1:35). These moments matter deeply. They train attention and quiet distraction. But withdrawal is not the secret place itself; it is a doorway into awareness.

The goal is not to find God in a room, but to recognise Him everywhere. This is why God speaks through the heart: "My son, give Me your heart" (Proverbs 23:26). The heart is the center of awareness. When the heart turns toward God, the secret place is present.

Over time, believers begin to realise something important: they are not entering and exiting God's presence. They are becoming aware or unaware of what is already true.

This removes striving from prayer. It replaces it with awareness. Jesus expresses this simply: "Abide in Me" (John 15:4). Abiding is not movement. It is remaining connected. A branch does not search for the vine. It lives from it. In the same way, the believer is not trying to reach God. They are learning to remain aware of Him.

Even emotional experience is no longer the measure. There are times of strong feeling and times of silence, but awareness is anchored in truth: "The Lord is near to all who call upon Him" (Psalm 145:18). Not sometimes near. Always near.

Stillness becomes important again, not as escape but as recognition. "Be still, and know that I am God" (Psalm 46:10). Stillness is where awareness is restored. Over time, something changes: scripture becomes encounter; prayer becomes awareness; worship becomes response; and silence becomes fellowship.

The secret place is no longer a destination. It becomes a way of life. David expresses this maturity: “I have set the Lord always before me” (Psalm 16:8).

Not occasionally. Always.

And when this becomes real in the heart, intimacy is no longer dependent on external conditions, because the believer realises: God was never far.

The secret place was never a place to find.

It was awareness being formed all along.

CHAPTER NINE

Learning To Recognize God's Voice

At a point in a believer's journey, something begins to shift quietly within the inner life. It is not always dramatic, nor is it easy to describe, yet it is deeply important. Prayer begins to feel less like speaking into the distance and more like responding to Someone already present. Scripture begins to feel less like reading information and more like encountering a living voice behind the words. In that quiet unfolding, a question begins to rise within the heart: How do I recognise the voice of God?

This question is not a sign of spiritual failure. It is often a sign of spiritual awakening. Because the desire to recognise God's voice is itself evidence that the heart is becoming more sensitive to Him. Jesus says something very simple, but deeply foundational: "My sheep hear My voice, and I know them, and they follow Me" (John 10:27). He does not say they might hear. He does not say only a few hear. He describes hearing as the normal reality for those who belong to Him.

But what does it mean to hear His voice in a life filled with noise, thoughts, emotions, responsibilities, and internal conflict? How does a believer learn to recognise what is from God and what is simply from their own mind, from external influence, or from an emotional reaction?

This is where many believers become uncertain, not because God is silent, but because discernment is not yet fully developed. It is important to begin with a stabilising truth: God is not distant or unwilling to speak. Scripture consistently reveals a speaking God. From the beginning, God speaks creation into existence. "And God said…" is the repeated pattern in Genesis. Creation itself begins with divine speech.

This means that communication is not something God occasionally does; it is part of who He is revealed to be.

Even in the life of Jesus, we see a consistent awareness of the Father's voice. He says, "The words that I speak to you I do not speak on My own authority; but the Father who dwells in Me does the works" (John 14:10). There is an ongoing relational awareness of communication between the Father and the Son.

So the issue is never whether God speaks.

The real question is whether the heart has learned to recognise His voice.

Recognition is different from hearing. Many sounds can be heard, but not all are recognised. Recognition implies familiarity. It implies a relationship formed over time. It implies repeated exposure until distinction becomes clear.

This is why Jesus uses the language of sheep and shepherd. Sheep do not analyse the shepherd's voice intellectually. They recognise it relationally. It is familiarity built through closeness, not theory built through study. This is what Jesus points to when He says, "My sheep hear My voice."

This means that hearing God is not first a skill to master but a relationship to grow in. At the beginning of the journey, a believer may struggle to distinguish their own thoughts from God's leading. This is normal. The inner life is often crowded at the start. Thoughts come quickly. Emotions shift. Internal dialogue is active. In such a space, clarity is not immediate.

But God does not abandon the believer in this process. Instead, He begins to cultivate sensitivity over time. One of the primary ways God develops this sensitivity is through Scripture. "All Scripture is given by inspiration of God" (2 Timothy 3:16).

The word “inspiration” here carries the idea of breath. Scripture is God-breathed. This means that the written Word carries the character, tone, and nature of God’s voice. As a believer becomes more familiar with Scripture, they become more attuned to the way God speaks. Not because Scripture replaces hearing, but because Scripture forms recognition.

The more the heart is saturated with the Word of God, the more readily it recognises what aligns with God’s nature and what does not. This is why the psalmist says, “Your word is a lamp to my feet and a light to my path” (Psalm 119:105). Light does not force direction. It reveals clarity.

But recognition of God’s voice is not formed only through reading Scripture. It is also shaped in the quiet process of a relationship. Jesus says, “When He, the Spirit of truth, has come, He will guide you into all truth” (John 16:13).

The Holy Spirit is not only present in moments of worship or prayer gatherings. He is actively involved in guiding the believer inwardly into truth. This guidance is not always loud. Often, it is subtle. A conviction that settles in the heart. A clarity that rises within. A sense of alignment or a warning that is difficult to fully explain yet deeply felt within the spirit.

However, this is where many believers become confused, because not every internal impression is from God. Human thoughts, emotions, and memories exist, as do external influences. So, learning to recognise God's voice requires not only sensitivity but also discernment.

Discernment grows through relationship.

Over time, a believer begins to notice a pattern. God's voice carries a certain consistency. It does not contradict Scripture. It does not lead to confusion or contradict His character.

It often carries peace, even when it brings correction. It may challenge the heart, but it does not destroy it. "Let the peace of God rule in your hearts" (Colossians 3:15). The word "rule" here implies acting as an umpire, helping to determine what is right and what is not.

This means peace is not a passive emotion; it is an indicator of alignment.

As the believer grows, they begin to recognise that God's voice is not always separate from thought, yet it is distinct. It often brings clarity rather than confusion. It often aligns with Scripture rather than contradicts it. It often draws the heart towards obedience rather than hesitation rooted in fear. But beyond these patterns, the deepest way to learn God's voice is simply to walk with Him over time.

Because recognition is not built in moments, it is built in relationships.

A believer who walks closely with God begins to recognise how He leads them personally, not in abstract ways but in lived experience. They notice how God gently redirects them, how He convicts without condemnation, how He leads without confusion, and how He corrects without destroying the heart.

This is why Scripture says, “The steps of a good man are ordered by the Lord” (Psalm 37:23). Steps are not leaps. They are gradual directions, one moment leading to the next.

Learning to recognise God’s voice is often not about dramatic instructions. It is about learning to follow small inner promptings of alignment over time. There are moments when the believer senses a quiet correction within, not audible, not external, but inward clarity that something is not aligned. There are moments when Scripture suddenly becomes alive in a personal way, as if it is addressing a current situation directly.

There are moments when prayer shifts from speaking to listening, and in that listening, clarity emerges. These are not unusual experiences reserved for a few. They are part of the normal development of intimacy with God.

But they require stillness to recognise.

This is why Scripture again returns to stillness: “Be still, and know that I am God” (Psalm 46:10). Stillness is not the absence of thought. It is the surrender of internal noise so that what God is already communicating can be perceived clearly. Without stillness, everything becomes noise. With stillness, distinction becomes possible.

And over time, something beautiful begins to happen.

The believer begins to trust God’s voice more than internal uncertainty. Not because they are never unsure, but because they have learned through relationships that His leading is faithful.

This is how trust is formed, not through theory but through repeated experience of God's faithfulness in guiding. Jesus says, "My sheep follow Me, for they know My voice" (John 10:4). Following comes from recognition. Recognition comes from a relationship. Relationship comes from time.

So, learning to recognise God's voice is not a sudden breakthrough. It is a slow formation of intimacy in which the heart becomes familiar with Him. And in that familiarity, fear diminishes.

Confusion diminishes.

Uncertainty reduces.

Because the believer is no longer trying to guess God. They are learning to know Him. And knowing Him becomes the foundation of hearing Him.

This is the quiet miracle of intimacy. God does not become louder.

The heart becomes more familiar.

CHAPTER TEN

The Weight of Silence

There is a part of the journey with God that many believers do not expect when they first pursue intimacy. It is not loud. It is not dramatic. It does not carry the emotional intensity that early encounters with God sometimes bring. Instead, it feels like an absence.

Silence.

And for many hearts, silence feels like distance.

A believer who has begun to grow in prayer, who has tasted moments of clarity, warmth, conviction, and awareness of God's presence, will eventually encounter seasons when those same feelings seem diminished. Prayer feels quieter. Scripture feels less emotionally immediate. The sense of God's nearness does not disappear; it simply becomes less emotionally expressive.

In these moments, a question often rises quietly within the heart: *Where is God?*

This question is not rebellion. It is often vulnerable. It comes from a heart that has tasted nearness and now feels the absence of its emotional expression. But one of the most important lessons in intimacy with God is this: silence does not mean absence.

Scripture is not silent about silence. In fact, it repeatedly shows us that God often forms depth in the believer not through constant expression, but through seasons when He seems quiet. David expresses this tension honestly when he cries, "Why do You stand far off, O Lord? Why do You hide Yourself in times of trouble?" (Psalm 10:1). This is not a statement of unbelief.

It is a moment of emotional honesty within a relationship. David is not speaking about God as a stranger. He is speaking to God as someone he still trusts, even amid confusion. This is an important distinction. Silence does not end a relationship. It reveals what kind of relationship exists.

If a relationship is sustained only by emotional feedback, silence feels like loss. But if a relationship is rooted in covenant, silence becomes a different kind of space. It becomes a place where trust is refined. The believer begins to learn something that cannot be learned in emotional highs: God is not only present when He is felt.

Scripture affirms this in a quiet but powerful way: "The just shall live by faith" (Habakkuk 2:4). Faith is not the same as feeling. Faith continues where feeling is not leading.

This is where silence becomes weighty.

Because silence removes the emotional support structures many believers did not realise they were leaning on. When God feels strongly present, prayer feels easier. When Scripture feels alive with emotion, reading feels effortless. But in silence, those emotional supports are weaker. And in that space, something deeper is being formed.

Faith that is not dependent on sensation.

Silence is not God withdrawing. Silence is often God's deepening. Intimacy cannot mature if it depends only on emotional confirmation. If a believer believes God is near only when they feel it, their relationship with God remains dependent on fluctuation. But God is leading believers into something more stable than emotion.

He is forming awareness.

This is why Scripture says, “We walk by faith, not by sight” (2 Corinthians 5:7).

Sight includes what is seen and what is felt. Faith continues beyond both. In silence, the believer begins to learn to remain with God without emotional reinforcement. They begin to discover that prayer is not only communication when it feels alive, but also trust when it feels quiet.

This is where depth begins to form in the soul. Silence confronts something very real within human nature: the desire for constant confirmation. Many believers are comfortable with God when His presence feels clear and expressive. But silence tests whether the relationship remains when expression is weak.

Jesus Himself experienced silence in a profound moment on the cross when He cried, "My God, My God, why have You forsaken Me?" (Matthew 27:46). This moment is not evidence of a broken relationship within the Trinity, but it reveals something about human experience of divine silence.

Even the Son, in His human expression, enters the depths of felt absence. Yet even in that moment, the relationship was not broken. This is important for the believer to understand: silence is not rejection.

Silence is not abandonment.

Silence is not withdrawal of love.

Silence is often the place where love becomes deeper than feeling. Love that depends only on emotional expression is still immature. But love that remains even when expression is quiet begins to become stable. This is why Scripture says, “Be still, and know that I am God” (Psalm 46:10). Stillness is not only external quietness.

It is an internal surrender in the absence of noise. It is the decision to remain with God even when nothing seems to be happening. Silence creates a space where motives are revealed. It exposes what the believer truly seeks in God.

Is it only experience? Is it only an emotional encounter? Or is it God Himself? In silence, many believers discover that their pursuit of God has sometimes been intertwined with the pursuit of feeling. This is not a condemnation. It is exposure for refinement. God is not trying to remove desire. He is purifying it.

This is why silence often feels uncomfortable. It removes what is familiar, slows what is expected, and strips away emotional certainty so that something deeper can emerge: trust.

Trust that does not rely on sensation.

Trust that does not depend on clarity of feeling.

Trust that remains anchored in the relationship. David again gives language to this kind of trust when he says, "Though I walk through the valley of the shadow of death, I will fear no evil, for You are with me" (Psalm 23:4).

Notice carefully: awareness of God's presence is not based on visible proof but on relational confidence. "You are with me" is not a statement of feeling. It is a statement of relationship.

Silence teaches this kind of knowing.

Over time, the believer comes to realise that silence is not empty. It is full of information. It is where endurance is shaped. It is where trust is strengthened. It is where dependence is purified from emotional demand into relational stability.

In silence, prayer changes.

It becomes less about expression and more about staying.

Less about hearing an immediate response and more about remaining in a relationship.

This is where intimacy begins to mature beyond its early stages. Early intimacy often depends on emotional awareness of God, but mature intimacy continues even when that awareness is quiet. This is not dryness. This is depth forming in hidden ways.

Even when the believer feels little, something is happening within them. Their dependence on God is being strengthened. Their awareness is being refined. Their faith is being stabilised.

This is why silence is not wasted time.

It is formation time.

The believer who endures silence without abandoning the relationship often emerges with deeper stability in God than before. Not because silence is pleasant, but because it becomes meaningful in hindsight. They begin to understand that God was not absent.

He was forming something that noise could not produce. In that realisation, silence loses its fear.

It becomes understood.

Not fully explained.

But deeply trusted.

Because intimacy with God is not built only in moments of felt presence. It is also built on seasons of quiet trust. And sometimes the deepest work God does in a believer is not when He speaks loudly. But when He seems silent, and yet remains near.

CHAPTER ELEVEN

When God Seems Distant

There are seasons in the life of a believer when the most honest description of their inner experience is not confusion about doctrine, but confusion about presence. They still believe God is real. They still believe His Word is true. They still pray, read Scripture, and attend gatherings of believers. Yet something within feels unfamiliar. Not rebellion. Not denial. But a quiet sense of distance that is difficult to explain.

In these seasons, a question rises from deep within the human spirit: Where is God?

This question has been asked by believers across generations. It is neither new nor strange. It is part of the lived reality of a relationship that is deeper than emotion.

Intimacy with God is formed not only in moments of felt closeness but also in seasons when closeness is not emotionally apparent.

Scripture does not ignore this experience. In fact, it gives it language. David cries out, “My God, my God, why have You forsaken me? Why are You so far from helping me?” (Psalm 22:1). These words are not written by someone who has abandoned God. They are written by someone who is still speaking to God amid felt distance. The relationship has not ended; the feeling of nearness has changed.

This distinction is critical.

Feeling distant is not the same as being distant.

God’s presence is not determined by emotional awareness. It is determined by His nature. “I will never leave you nor forsake you” (Hebrews 13:5).

This is not a conditional statement based on perception. It is a covenant declaration rooted in God's character. Yet human experience is real. The believer does not live only in theological truth; they also live in emotional awareness. Sometimes these two seem to contradict each other. The truth says God is near. The feeling says He is far. The Word says He is present. The experience feels silent.

It is in this tension that faith is formed at a deeper level.

Because faith is not only believing what is visible or felt. Faith is remaining anchored in what God has said, even when experience does not immediately align with it. "We walk by faith, not by sight" (2 Corinthians 5:7). Here, sight includes not only physical vision but also internal perception, emotional awareness, and sensory confirmation.

So, when God seems distant, the believer is invited into a deeper form of trust.

This is where many misunderstand the nature of spiritual growth. They assume that nearness to God should always feel consistent. Yet Scripture reveals a different pattern. There are moments of clarity, silence, intensity, and hiddenness. All of these are part of formation.

Isaiah speaks of a season when God says, "Truly You are a God who hides Yourself, O God of Israel, the Saviour" (Isaiah 45:15). This is a startling statement. It does not say God is absent. It says He hides Himself. Hiding is not abandonment. It is intentional concealment for deeper purposes.

A hidden God is still a present God.

But hiddenness changes how He is sought.

It forces the heart to move beyond emotional dependence into relational depth. When God feels distant, the believer often begins to search more earnestly.

Prayer becomes less about routine and more about pursuit. Scripture becomes less about reading and more about seeking. Worship becomes less about expression and more about reaching. This is because emotional distance often intensifies desire in the heart.

David captures this tension when he says, "As the deer pants for the water brooks, so my soul pants for You, O God" (Psalm 42:1). Notice the language: panting. This is not casual devotion. This is a deep longing that arises when something essential feels less accessible. Yet even in this longing, David continues to speak to God. He does not disconnect. He does not walk away. He wrestles within a relationship.

This is important.

Spiritual maturity is not the absence of tension. It is the ability to remain in a relationship under tension.

When God seems distant, one of the greatest dangers is misinterpretation. The believer may assume that a lack of feeling reflects a lack of reality. Yet Scripture consistently corrects this assumption. “Where can I go from Your Spirit? Or where can I flee from Your presence?” (Psalm 139:7). The answer is given throughout the passage: nowhere. Not because the believer always feels Him, but because He is everywhere present.

This means the experience of distance is not geographical or relational separation. It is perceptual. Something in inner awareness has shifted, not God’s position. This is why seasons of distance are often seasons of formation. They expose what the believer truly relies on. If intimacy with God is sustained only by feeling, then when feeling changes, stability is shaken. But if intimacy is rooted in covenant, then feeling becomes secondary to truth.

God often uses these seasons to deepen that stability. Because he is not only building closeness, he is also building maturity. There is a difference between being carried by experience and being anchored in a relationship. When God seems distant, the believer is being trained to anchor more deeply.

Jesus Himself enters into the depth of perceived distance in His humanity when He cries from the cross, “My God, My God, why have You forsaken Me?” (Matthew 27:46). In that moment, the feeling of separation is expressed. Yet even there, He speaks to God. The relationship is not broken even when the experience of closeness is overshadowed.

This reveals something profound: a relationship with God is strong enough to hold even in perceived distance.

So, what is God doing in these seasons?

He is strengthening trust beyond emotion.

He is forming reliance beyond sensation.

He is building intimacy that does not collapse when feelings shift.

Feelings do shift.

But God does not.

This is why Scripture says, "Jesus Christ is the same yesterday, today, and forever" (Hebrews 13:8). The constancy is not in human awareness. It is in His nature.

As the believer walks through seasons when God seems distant, something begins to unfold within them. They notice that although feelings fluctuate, God's faithfulness does not. Although awareness changes, His presence remains steady. Although emotions rise and fall, His Word does not move.

This begins to reshape how they interpret silence, delay, and distance.

What once felt like absence begins to be understood as a hidden presence. What once felt like withdrawal begins to be understood as a deeper formation. What once felt like separation begins to be understood as an invitation into trust.

This does not remove the ache, but it gives it meaning.

And meaning changes endurance.

The believer begins to pray differently in these seasons. Not always with intensity of feeling, but with persistence of trust. Not always with emotional clarity, but with relational commitment. Not always with a visible response, but with inward anchoring. This is where intimacy becomes more mature than experience.

Because intimacy is no longer dependent on how close God feels.

It is grounded in who God is.

And who He is does not change.

So even when He seems distant, the believer learns to say, not always with emotion but with conviction: You are still here.

This is the quiet strength that grows in seasons of perceived distance.

Not emotional certainty.

But relational trust.

And in time, the believer often looks back and realises something they could not see in the moment: God was not absent at all.

He was forming something in them that nearness alone could not produce.

He was teaching them how to remain.

PART III

DEEPENING PRAYER LIFE

CHAPTER TWELVE

The Purification of Motives in Prayer

There is a stage in the journey of prayer that every sincere believer eventually encounters, though not everyone recognises it when it begins. It is not marked by new vocabulary or greater spiritual activity. It is marked by something far more internal and unsettling. It is the moment when prayer begins to expose the heart that is praying.

At first, prayer feels simple. The believer comes before God with requests, needs, desires, burdens, and hopes. There is sincerity in this stage. There is faith. There is dependence. Scripture encourages this openness: "Let your requests be made known to God" (Philippians 4:6).

God does not reject the voice of need. He invites it.

But as the believer continues to walk with God, something deeper begins to happen that they did not anticipate. Prayer stops being only about what is asked for and begins to reveal why it is asked.

This is where motives begin to surface.

Not in accusation, but in awareness.

Not in condemnation, but in clarity.

The believer begins to notice that beneath some prayers lie layers of desire that were not fully seen before. Some desires are pure and aligned with God's will. Others are mixed with fear, insecurity, ambition, comparison, or the need for control. And in this moment, prayer becomes something different. It becomes a place of exposure.

This is not because God has changed. It is because intimacy has increased.

The closer the believer draws to God, the more light there is in the inner life. And light always reveals what was previously hidden.

Scripture describes God in this way: "The word of God is living and powerful, and sharper than any two-edged sword… and is a discerner of the thoughts and intents of the heart" (Hebrews 4:12). Notice carefully that it discerns not only actions but also intentions.

This is where prayer begins to deepen beyond asking. The believer is no longer only speaking to God; they are being formed by Him in the process of speaking.

At this stage, many believers experience a subtle discomfort. Not because God is rejecting them, but because their inner world is being rearranged. Prayers that once felt clear now feel more complex. Requests that once felt certain now feel questioned—not by God in harshness, but by truth in light.

Why do I want this?

What am I really seeking?

Is this desire rooted in love for God or in love for the outcome?

These questions arise naturally, not as an external interrogation but as an internal awareness.

This is the beginning of purification.

Jesus speaks to this deeper layer of prayer when He says, "Seek first the kingdom of God and His righteousness, and all these things shall be added to you" (Matthew 6:33). The order is not accidental. It signals a reorientation of desire. What is primary and what is secondary must be rearranged.

Many believers begin their prayer life with "these things" at the centre. Needs. Outcomes. Solutions. Changes. But intimacy gradually shifts the centre towards the kingdom itself, towards God's will, God's presence, God's nature.

This shift does not happen instantly. It unfolds through encounter, time, correction, silence, delay, answered prayer, and unanswered expectation. All of these become tools in God's hands, not to harm the believer but to purify desire. God is not only interested in giving answers. He is interested in forming sons and daughters whose desires reflect His heart.

This is why Scripture says, "Delight yourself in the Lord, and He will give you the desires of your heart" (Psalm 37:4). This verse is often misunderstood. It does not mean God simply fulfils whatever the heart naturally wants. It means that as the heart delights in God, its desires are reshaped to align with Him.

Desire itself becomes transformed.

In this process, prayer begins to change tone.

The believer may still ask, but asking becomes less driven by anxiety and more anchored in trust. There is less desperation for control and more surrender to God's wisdom. There is less insistence on specific outcomes and more openness to divine direction.

This is not passivity. It is purification.

Because surrender is not the absence of desire. It is the alignment of desire.

This is where the Holy Spirit becomes deeply active in the believer's inner life. Jesus says of Him, "He will convict the world of sin, and of righteousness, and of judgment" (John 16:8). Conviction is not rejection. It is alignment. It is the gentle but firm work of bringing the heart into agreement with truth.

Sometimes this conviction comes through Scripture. A verse suddenly speaks directly into a hidden motive. Sometimes it comes through a delay. Sometimes through closed doors. Sometimes through silence.

Sometimes, answered prayer reveals something about the heart that asked. And in all of it, God is not pushing the believer away. He is drawing them closer to the truth. Because intimacy cannot remain shallow. It cannot remain mixed indefinitely. At some point, love begins to refine love.

This is why the believer begins to notice that God is not only answering prayers; He is shaping the one who prays.

And this shaping often feels like exposure.

But exposure is not rejection.

It is an invitation to clarity.

David expresses this openness when he says, "Search me, O God, and know my heart… and see if there is any wicked way in me, and lead me in the way everlasting" (Psalm 139:23–24). This is not a fearful prayer. It is a surrendered one. David is not hiding from God's examination; he is inviting it.

This is the posture that develops in true intimacy. Not defensiveness. Not self-protection. But openness. As the believer comes to understand that God's purification is not against them but for them, He removes what distorts desire, leaving what remains pure and aligned.

Over time, something beautiful begins to emerge.

Prayer becomes less crowded with mixed motives. Desire becomes clearer. The heart becomes less divided. There is still longing, but it is less anxious. There is still asking, but it is more of a surrender. There is still expectation, but it is held within trust.

This is the fruit of purification.

Not the removal of desire, but the alignment of desire.

Jesus describes this inner simplicity when He says, "Blessed are the pure in heart, for they shall see God" (Matthew 5:8).

Purity here is not perfection; it is clarity. A heart that is no longer divided in its pursuit. And seeing God is not only for the future. It is present awareness. It is recognition. It is intimacy. So, purification is not God stripping the believer of joy.

It is God removing the distortion so joy can become stable. Because a heart that is divided cannot sustain intimacy. But a heart that is aligned can remain in nearness. And this is where the believer begins to discover something they did not expect:

The more purified their motives become, the simpler prayer becomes. And the simpler the prayer becomes, the deeper the intimacy becomes. Because now the heart is no longer pulled in multiple directions.

It rests in one desire.

God Himself.

CHAPTER THIRTEEN

Prayer That Agrees with God

There comes a moment in the believer's journey when prayer begins to feel different, not because the words have become more eloquent, but because the heart has begun to shift its centre. It is not that the believer stops asking. It is not that needs disappear.

Life still presents questions, responsibilities, uncertainties, and burdens. But something deeper begins to form beneath the surface of prayer.

The direction of prayer slowly changes.

At first, prayer often moves outward from the believer towards God, with a desire for God to respond. This is natural. It is how many begin their walk with Him. Needs arise, and the heart reaches upwards.

Scripture affirms this openness: "Call upon Me in the day of trouble; I will deliver you" (Psalm 50:15). God invites the cries of His people. But as intimacy deepens, prayer begins to undergo a quiet transformation. The believer comes to realise that prayer is not only about bringing requests before God, but also about aligning with what God already desires.

This is where agreement begins.

Agreement with God is not a replacement for prayer. It is the maturation of prayer. Jesus reveals this when He teaches His disciples to pray, "Your kingdom come. Your will be done on earth as it is in heaven" (Matthew 6:10). This is not a passive statement. It is a realignment of desire. The centre of prayer shifts from "what I want changed" to "what You are doing being established."

This does not mean personal desires are erased. It means they are being reshaped within a larger reality, the will of God.

At this stage of spiritual growth, something begins to happen within the believer that is difficult to describe in purely emotional terms. Prayer begins to lose some of its internal resistance. There is less struggle to convince God, less urgency to persuade, and greater willingness to understand. The heart settles into trust.

This is not a resignation. It is an agreement.

There is a difference between giving up and yielding. Giving up disconnects from hope. Yielding remains in the relationship but releases control. This is where Scripture begins to take deeper root in the believer's inner life. "For My thoughts are not your thoughts, nor are your ways My ways," says the Lord (Isaiah 55:8).

This is not a statement meant to distance the believer from God, but to reframe understanding. God is not confused about His direction. He is not uncertain about His purpose. His wisdom extends beyond immediate perception.

Agreement with God begins when the believer stops interpreting God's will only through the lens of personal expectation. Instead of asking, "Why is this not happening the way I expected?" the heart begins to ask, "What is God doing that I may not yet see?"

This is a subtle but profound shift.

It is the beginning of trust that is not dependent on immediate clarity.

Paul expresses something similar when he writes, "We know that all things work together for good to those who love God, to those who are called according to His purpose" (Romans 8:28). Notice carefully, this is not a statement that all things feel good. It is a statement that God is at work within all things.

Agreement with God begins when the believer starts to trust His activity, even when His process is not fully understood.

Here, prayer begins to shift in tone. It becomes less argumentative in spirit and more receptive in posture. There is still honesty. There is still wrestling at times. Scripture does not hide this. Even Jesus, in Gethsemane, says, “My Father, if it is possible, let this cup pass from Me; nevertheless, not as I will, but as You will” (Matthew 26:39). This is not a denial of desire. It is a surrender of control.

This moment is central to understanding agreement with God. It shows that alignment does not mean the absence of human feeling. It means submitting human will to divine wisdom.

There is a depth to prayer that emerges only when the believer begins to trust God’s will more than their own interpretation of what should happen. This is not easy. It often develops over time, through experiences when outcomes do not match expectations, through seasons of waiting, through moments of silence, and through encounters with God that reshape understanding.

But slowly, something beautiful begins to form.

The believer begins to realise that God is not only interested in giving answers; He is forming an agreement. Agreement is deeper than a request. A request asks God to change something. Agreement aligns with what God is already doing.

This does not remove the believer's voice in prayer. It refines it. The believer still speaks, still brings burdens, still expresses desire. But beneath it all, there is a growing surrender that says, "Lord, I want what You want more than I want my own outcome."

This is not passivity. It is intimacy reaching maturity.

Because intimacy is not only about closeness. It is about alignment.

Two lives drawing so close that their desires begin to reflect one another.

Scripture describes this transformation when it says, “Delight yourself in the Lord, and He will give you the desires of your heart” (Psalm 37:4). As the believer delights in God, desire itself is reshaped. The heart begins to want differently, not by force but by exposure to God’s nature.

This is how agreement is formed, not through pressure but through relationship.

The more time the believer spends in awareness of God, the more their inner life begins to adjust. What once felt urgent begins to feel secondary, and what once felt central begins to shift. Not because life stops mattering, but because God becomes the interpretive centre of life.

At this stage, prayer begins to carry a quiet stability. There is less inner conflict between what is desired and what is surrendered. Even in uncertainty, there is a growing sense of trust that God is not absent from the process.

This is where peace begins to deepen.

Paul describes this reality when he writes, "And the peace of God, which surpasses all understanding, will guard your hearts and minds through Christ Jesus" (Philippians 4:7). This peace is not dependent on outcomes. It is rooted in alignment.

Agreement with God produces peace, not because everything is resolved, but because the heart is no longer in opposition to His will. This is one of the most important shifts in prayer life. Opposition creates internal tension, even in prayer. But agreement creates rest within movement.

The believer is still praying. Still asking. Still seeking. But now there is a deeper layer beneath all expression: trust in God's wisdom. As this trust grows, something begins to happen that cannot be manufactured. The believer begins to pray less out of anxiety and more out of a relationship.

Less from urgency alone, more from alignment. Less from fear of missing out, more from confidence in God's timing. This is where prayer becomes less about trying to convince God and more about walking with God. Agreement does not silence desire. It places desire under trust.

It does not remove questions. It brings them into a relationship.

It does not eliminate waiting. It transforms waiting into participation in God's process.

Over time, the believer comes to realise something they did not see at the beginning of their journey: that God was not only listening to their prayers but shaping their heart through them. And in that realisation, prayer itself becomes something deeper than communication.

It becomes a formation.

And agreement with God becomes the place where the heart finds rest, not because everything is understood, but because God is trusted.

CHAPTER FOURTEEN

The Quiet Transformation of Desire

There is a kind of change in the believer's life that does not announce itself loudly. It does not arrive with sudden interruption or dramatic emotional shifts. It comes quietly, almost unnoticed at first, until one day the believer realises that something within them no longer responds to life as it once did.

Desire begins to change.

Not disappear. Not weaken. But change in direction, in weight, in centre.

At the beginning of the journey with God, desire is often immediate and visible. The believer knows what they want. They know what they are asking for in prayer.

They know what they hope will change, what they hope will open, what they hope will be resolved. These desires are often sincere. They are not fake or shallow. They are human.

God does not reject human desire. Scripture does not present God as distant from human longing. Rather, He engages with it. “Delight yourself in the Lord, and He will give you the desires of your heart” (Psalm 37:4). This verse reveals something important: desire is not removed in relationship with God; it is reshaped.

But reshaping takes time.

And it is rarely noticed in the moment.

At first, the believer prays for what they want with clarity. But as intimacy with God deepens, something begins to happen beneath the surface. Certain desires begin to feel heavier than before. Not necessarily wrong, but more complex.

Other desires begin to lose their urgency. Things that once felt central become less consuming. This is not emotional burnout. It is spiritual reordering, because nearness to God not only changes behaviour. It changes appetite.

Scripture speaks to this quietly yet powerfully: “As newborn babes, desire the pure milk of the word, that you may grow thereby” (1 Peter 2:2). Growth in God is not only about what is done externally. It is about what is desired internally.

Desire is not static. It is formed, shaped, and refined over time.

This is where many believers begin to notice something unexpected: prayer begins to affect what they want. At first, they came to prayer with desires already formed. But over time, prayer begins to shape those desires.

This is one of the most intimate works. Intimacy with God is not only about receiving what the heart already wants. It is about the heart learning to want differently. This is not suppression of desire. It is a transformation of desire.

The Holy Spirit plays a central role in this inward work. Jesus says of Him, “He will take of what is Mine and declare it to you” (John 16:14). The Spirit not only informs the believer. He forms the believer. He brings alignment between the heart of God and the heart of the believer.

This is often experienced in subtle ways. A believer may find that something they once pursued strongly no longer carries the same emotional pull. Or they may find themselves drawn toward things they previously overlooked, quiet obedience, hidden faithfulness, deeper prayer, patience, and surrender.

These shifts are not forced. They are formed. Because they unfold slowly, they are often recognised only in hindsight. One of the clearest signs of this transformation is that prayer begins to lose its anxious urgency. Not its honesty, but its anxiety. The believer still brings desires before God, but something within them begins to rest more deeply in His presence even before outcomes are known.

This is because desire is no longer the sole driving force in prayer. Awareness of God has moved to the centre.

And awareness changes desire.

When a believer is far from God in awareness, desire often grows louder. It demands attention. It pushes for fulfilment. It becomes urgent because it is disconnected from presence. But when a believer draws nearer to God, desire begins to be held within a relationship.

It is no longer isolated.

It is no longer alone.

It is now held in communion.

This is where transformation begins.

Jesus gives language to this deeper reality when He says, “Seek first the kingdom of God and His righteousness” (Matthew 6:33). Seeking first is not only about priority in action. It is about priority in desire. What is first in the heart begins to reshape everything that follows. At this stage, the believer begins to notice that God is not only answering prayers; He is refining what is prayed for.

This can feel uncomfortable at times because refinement exposes mixed motives, unclear desires, and internal contradictions. But it is not a condemnation. It is purification.

The heart begins to see itself more clearly in the light of God’s presence.

David experienced this when he prayed, “Search me, O God, and know my heart… and see if there is any wicked way in me” (Psalm 139:23–24). This is not fear-based prayer. It is an invitation to surrender. David is not avoiding examination; he is welcoming it.

Because intimacy produces a heart that no longer fears alignment with God.

As desire begins to transform, something else happens quietly. The believer begins to want God Himself more than what God gives.

This is a significant shift.

Because early in the journey, what God gives often feels like the primary evidence of His goodness. But as intimacy deepens, God Himself becomes the centre of desire.

This does not mean blessings lose meaning. It means they lose centrality.

Paul describes this transformation in his own life when he says, "Indeed I also count all things loss for the excellence of the knowledge of Christ Jesus my Lord" (Philippians 3:8). Notice carefully that the value system has shifted, not because things are evil, but because Christ has become weightier than everything else.

This is the quiet transformation of desire.

It is not dramatic on the surface, yet it is profound in depth.

The believer still lives in the world. They still experience needs. They still have responsibilities, hopes, and longings. But the centre has changed. God is no longer only the One who responds to desire. He is the One who shapes it.

And this is where deeper stability begins to form, because desires shaped by God are less fragile than those shaped only by circumstance. They are not easily shaken.

They are not easily lost.

They are rooted in a relationship.

Over time, the believer comes to realise something subtle yet important: some of the prayers once offered with intensity are no longer prayed in the same way. Not because God rejected them, but because God reshaped the heart that prayed them.

And in that reshaping, peace begins to grow.

Not because everything is fulfilled.

But because everything is aligned.

This is why Scripture says, "Great peace have those who love Your law, and nothing causes them to stumble" (Psalm 119:165). Peace here is not the absence of desire. It is the presence of alignment. When desire is transformed, peace deepens.

Because conflict within the heart diminishes.

Not because life becomes simpler, but because the inner world becomes ordered.

This is one of the quietest miracles of intimacy with God. He not only changes what is around the believer. He changes what is within the believer. And in that inner change, desire itself becomes a place of communion rather than conflict.

The believer no longer only brings desire to God.

They begin to discover that God is already present within the shaping of desire itself. And that is where transformation becomes complete. When desire is purified, prayer becomes simpler. When prayer becomes simpler, intimacy becomes deeper. As intimacy deepens, the heart no longer seeks only what God can do.

It seeks God Himself.

CHAPTER FIFTEEN

The Weight of God's Presence

There is a moment in a believer's journey when words begin to feel insufficient to describe what is happening within. Not because language has failed, but because experience has gone deeper than explanation can carry. The believer begins to realise that God is not only a concept to be understood or a subject to be studied, but a presence that can be known, encountered, and felt in the deepest part of human awareness.

Yet even this word, felt, does not fully capture it.

Because the presence of God is not only emotional, it is weighty.

Scripture gives us a word for this that many believers overlook in reading but experience deeply in encounter: glory.

The Hebrew word often associated with glory conveys weight, heaviness, and significance. When Scripture speaks of the glory of God filling a place, it is not describing something light or abstract. It is describing something substantial within spiritual reality.

When Solomon dedicated the temple, Scripture says, “The house of the Lord was filled with a cloud, so that the priests could not continue ministering… for the glory of the Lord filled the house of God” (2 Chronicles 5:13–14). There was something about the presence of God that interrupted normal activity, not through fear alone, but through an overwhelming reality.

This is important for the believer to understand: the presence of God is not only comforting. It is also weighty. There are dimensions of His nearness that produce peace, and there are dimensions that produce stillness. Not silence of absence, but silence of reverence.

As intimacy with God deepens, the believer begins to encounter this weight in ways that are difficult to describe yet impossible to ignore. It may come in moments of prayer, when words slow. Not because the mind is distracted, but because something deeper is unfolding in awareness. It may come in worship, where expression gives way to stillness.

It may come in Scripture, where a verse carries an internal gravity that settles beyond thought.

This is not emotional intensity alone. It is spiritual awareness of presence.

Moses experienced something similar when he encountered God on the mountain. Scripture says, "Moses made haste and bowed his head towards the earth, and worshipped" (Exodus 34:8). There was no argument, no delay, no negotiation. Encounter produced a response.

When the presence of God becomes weighty, human response becomes less mechanical and more surrendered, not because of pressure but because of awareness. Something within recognises that it stands before a reality greater than itself.

Isaiah also describes this encounter when he says, “I saw the Lord sitting on a throne, high and lifted up” (Isaiah 6:1). His immediate response is not curiosity but conviction. “Woe is me, for I am undone” (Isaiah 6:5). Again, this is not destruction in the sense of harm. It is the awareness of holiness that reveals human limitation.

The weight of God’s presence does not crush the believer in rejection. It exposes the believer in truth. And truth, when received in intimacy, becomes transformation.

Many believers first encounter God in gentle, comforting ways. And this is good.

God often begins with tenderness because the human heart must be drawn, not forced. "With lovingkindness I have drawn you" (Jeremiah 31:3). But as the relationship deepens, the believer comes to realise that God is not only gentle in presence; He is also holy in presence.

And holiness carries weight.

This weight is not oppressive. It is clarifying. It brings clarity to the inner world. Thoughts grow quieter. Motives become more visible. Distractions lose their hold. The heart becomes more aware of what is real and what is not.

This is why, in moments of deep encounter, many believers find they cannot remain unchanged in their posture, thoughts, or attitudes. Not because they are forced, but because awareness changes everything. The presence of God has a way of making the inner world more honest.

David expresses this awareness when he says, “Where can I go from Your Spirit? Or where can I flee from Your presence?” (Psalm 139:7). This is not fear of escape. It is recognition of inescapable nearness. God is not distant in those moments. He is overwhelmingly near.

And nearness carries weight.

As the believer grows in intimacy, they begin to recognise that this weight is not confined to specific moments such as worship services or prayer times. It can also become a quiet awareness that rests beneath ordinary life, a sense that God is not far removed from the details of living but present within them.

This awareness does not always produce emotion. Sometimes it produces stillness. Sometimes it produces reflection. Sometimes it produces a silence within the heart that is not emptiness but fullness too deep for words.

This is where the believer begins to understand something important: the presence of God is not always loud, but it is always real. Elijah discovered this on the mountain when God was not in the wind, not in the earthquake, and not in the fire, but in the "still, small voice" (1 Kings 19:12). The absence of dramatic expression did not mean the absence of presence. It revealed a different kind of encounter, one that required attentiveness rather than intensity.

This is where intimacy matures.

The early stages of spiritual experience often depend on intensity, but deeper stages depend on awareness. The weight of God's presence begins to shape the believer internally. It creates reverence where casualness once existed. It creates attentiveness where distraction once ruled. It creates depth where superficiality once felt normal.

This is not a religious performance. It is relational formation.

Over time, the believer begins to notice that even when not in formal prayer, there is a sense of God's nearness, not as a burden, but as a grounding reality. This does not interrupt life. It anchors it.

This is what Scripture means when it says, “The Lord is near to all who call upon Him” (Psalm 145:18). Nearness is not occasional. It is continuous.

But awareness of nearness is cultivated.

As awareness grows, the weight of His presence becomes less overwhelming and more familiar. Not because it becomes lighter in reality, but because the believer grows in capacity to bear it.

This is what intimacy does.

It enlarges the inner life.

It stretches spiritual capacity.

It deepens reverence without destroying peace.

There is a paradox here that only experience can teach: the weight of God's presence can produce both awe and peace at the same time. Awe because of His holiness. Peace because of His nearness. Isaiah experiences this tension when he is first undone in God's presence, then cleansed and sent. The same presence that exposes also restores. "Your iniquity is taken away, and your sin purged" (Isaiah 6:7). The weight that revealed his condition also prepared him for his assignment.

This is how God's presence works. It not only reveals. It restores. It does not only expose. It commissions.

As the believer continues in intimacy, they begin to realise that the weight of God's presence is not something to fear but something to treasure, for it is in that weight that life is rightly ordered. Values shift. Priorities realign. Desires are clarified. The heart becomes more stable, not less.

This is why Scripture says, "In Your presence is fullness of joy" (Psalm 16:11). Here, joy is not superficial happiness. It is deep stability in nearness.

In that stability, the believer begins to grasp something profound: the presence of God is not something to be visited. It is something to be lived within.

Not always felt dramatically.

But always real.

And increasingly known.

PART IV

MATURITY AND ABIDING

CHAPTER SIXTEEN

The Life That Flows from Nearness

There comes a point in a believer's walk with God when attention shifts. At first, the focus is often on how to pray, hear God, grow, and become more spiritually aware. There is hunger, and rightly so. Hunger is often the beginning of intimacy.

But as the journey deepens, something begins to change. The focus is no longer only on seeking moments with God, but on the life that flows from those moments. What was once an experience becomes a way of life. What was once an intentional pursuit becomes quiet continuity. The believer begins to notice that nearness to God is no longer confined to specific times or settings. It begins to shape ordinary life.

This is what Scripture describes when it says, "In Him we live and move and have our being" (Acts 17:28). This is not poetic exaggeration. It is a statement about spiritual reality. Life with God was never meant to be segmented into sacred and secular compartments. It was meant to become the atmosphere of existence.

At this stage, prayer does not disappear. Scripture does not lose importance. Worship does not become less meaningful. But they begin to flow from something deeper than effort. They begin to flow from nearness.

The believer begins to notice that their inner life has changed in ways that are not always dramatic but are deeply consistent. There is a quieter mind. A more settled heart. A growing awareness of God in ordinary moments. Not because life has become easier, but because awareness has deepened.

Jesus points to this kind of life when He says, "Abide in Me, and I in you… for without Me you can do nothing" (John 15:4–5). Abiding is not an occasional spiritual event. It is sustained relational dwelling, life lived in awareness of connection.

From that abiding, fruit begins to appear.

Not forced fruit. Not manufactured behaviour. But the natural expression of inner transformation.

Jesus continues, "He who abides in Me, and I in him, bears much fruit" (John 15:5). Notice the order carefully. Fruit is not the starting point. It is the result of remaining.

This is important because many believers try to produce spiritual fruit without understanding spiritual nearness. They focus on output before abiding. But Scripture reverses that order. Life flows from nearness, not towards it.

As intimacy with God deepens, the believer begins to notice changes in how they respond to life. Situations that once produced anxiety begin to prompt prayerful awareness rather than panic. Challenges that once felt overwhelming begin to be carried differently. Not because difficulty disappears, but because inner stability increases.

This is the quiet fruit of nearness.

The believer also begins to notice a change in desires, not only in prayer but in daily living. Things that once dominated attention begin to lose their hold, not through suppression, but through replacement. God's presence becomes more central than external validation. Peace becomes more valuable than recognition. Obedience becomes more desirable than control.

Paul describes this inward shift when he says, "The fruit of the Spirit is love, joy, peace..." (Galatians 5:22). These are not external achievements.

They are internal outcomes of life in the Spirit. They grow where the Spirit is welcomed, and nearness is sustained. This is why nearness matters so deeply. It is not only about spiritual experience. It is about the formation of life.

As the believer continues on this path, they begin to realise that God is not only shaping their prayer life; He is shaping their entire way of being in the world. How they speak, how they listen, how they respond, how they wait, how they forgive, how they endure, all of it begins to shift gradually.

Not through pressure.

But through presence.

There is a difference between trying to live rightly and being formed into right living. One is effort-driven. The other is relationship-driven.

Nearness produces formation.

Distance produces struggle.

This is why Scripture emphasises walking with God. “Enoch walked with God, and he was not, for God took him” (Genesis 5:24). Walking is not dramatic language. It denotes steady, consistent movement in a relationship. It suggests continuity, not an occasional encounter.

This is the life that flows from nearness.

It is not a life of constant emotional highs. It is a life of increasing spiritual stability.

It is not a life free from challenge. It is a life in which challenge is no longer interpreted as separation from God.

It is not a life in which God is found only in extraordinary moments. It is a life in which God is recognised in ordinary ones. This is one of the most profound changes intimacy brings: the believer begins to live with the awareness that God is present even when nothing “spiritual” is happening in the external sense.

A conversation. A decision. A moment of silence. A season of waiting. All begin to carry an awareness of God's nearness.

This is what it means for life itself to flow from relationship.

It is not compartmentalised spirituality.

It is an integrated existence.

Paul describes this integration when he says, "Whatever you do, do all to the glory of God" (1 Corinthians 10:31). This is not about performance. It is about orientation. Life becomes oriented towards God, not only in religious activity but in daily awareness.

As this deepens, something else begins to happen quietly within the believer. Their reactions begin to change. Not instantly, not perfectly, but noticeably. There is less impulsive reaction and more reflective response: less internal chaos and more internal awareness.

This is not a personality change. It is spiritual formation. Nearness not only changes what a person believes, but also shapes how a person believes. It changes how they carry themselves in life. There is also a growing simplicity that emerges. Not a simplification of life circumstances, but a simplification of inner focus. Fewer internal contradictions. Less divided attention. More clarity of direction.

Jesus expresses this simplicity when He says, "The lamp of the body is the eye. If therefore your eye is good, your whole body will be full of light" (Matthew 6:22). A unified inner focus produces clarity in life.

Nearness brings that kind of clarity.

Over time, the believer comes to understand deeply: life with God is not meant to be experienced only in moments of spiritual intensity. It is meant to become the steady background of all living.

Not always emotionally felt.

But spiritually real.

And relationally known.

This is the life that flows from nearness.

Not an escape from reality.

But deeper participation in it, with God present in every part.

CHAPTER SEVENTEEN

The Invitation That Never Ends

There is a common misunderstanding that often accompanies spiritual growth: the assumption that the journey with God becomes complete in a fixed sense, as though intimacy has a final destination where everything is settled, all questions are answered, and the pursuit concludes.

But Scripture does not describe the relationship with God in that way.

Instead, it describes a life of continuing nearness, continuing growth, and continuing invitation.

Even the most mature believers in Scripture do not speak as though they have arrived at the end of their journey in knowing God.

Paul, towards the end of his life, writes with striking humility: "That I may know Him"

(Philippians 3:10). He is already an apostle. Already experienced and already used by God in profound ways. Yet his language remains relational and ongoing. He does not speak as one who has finished knowing God, but as one still being drawn deeper.

This reveals something essential about intimacy: it is never static.

It does not end in possession. It continues in a relationship.

The invitation of God is not a one-off moment that leads to spiritual self-sufficiency. It is a continuous drawing of the heart into deeper awareness of Him. Jesus expresses this ongoing invitation when He says, “Abide in Me” (John 15:4). Abide is not a command that ends with obedience. It is a way of living that sustains itself through continued relationships.

This means that even after transformation, growth, and clarity, the believer still lives within an invitation. God is not only the One who called them at the beginning. He is the One who continues to call them deeper.

This is why intimacy cannot be reduced to achievement language. It is not something the believer completes like a task. It is something they continue to respond to, like a relationship that unfolds over time.

The danger of misunderstanding this is subtle. A believer may begin to think they have reached a point where pursuit is no longer necessary. But spiritual life does not work that way. The moment pursuit ends, awareness begins to dull. Not because God has moved, but because attention has shifted.

This is why Scripture repeatedly calls the believer to remain awake, attentive, and watchful. "Continue earnestly in prayer, being vigilant in it with thanksgiving" (Colossians 4:2). Continuity is part of spiritual life.

God's invitation is not exhausted by past encounters. Each encounter leads to a deeper invitation. Each revelation opens to further discovery. Each moment of nearness becomes a doorway to greater nearness.

This is the nature of God Himself: infinite in being, yet personal in relationship.

And because He is infinite, there is always more to know, not in a way that creates frustration, but in a way that sustains wonder.

One of the quiet signs of growing intimacy is not a reduction in desire for God, but a deepening awareness that He cannot be exhausted. The believer begins to realise that every season with God reveals something true, but never everything in full.

Even Moses, who spoke with God "face to face as a man speaks to his friend" (Exodus 33:11), still asks, "Show me Your glory" (Exodus 33:18).

Even in deep friendship, there remains a hunger for more revelation. This is not immaturity. It is the nature of a relationship with God.

The invitation never ends because God never becomes less than Himself. He is always revealing, always drawing, always inviting the heart further into Himself.

And this invitation is gentle.

It does not force. It calls.

It does not overwhelm. It draws.

Jesus says, "Behold, I stand at the door and knock" (Revelation 3:20). Even after salvation, even after growth, even after seasons of intimacy, the knocking continues, not because the believer is far away, but because God is always inviting deeper fellowship.

This is one of the most important truths for the believer to grasp: nearness to God is not a place where hunger ends. It is a place where hunger becomes deeper, purer, and more stable. The more the believer knows God, the more they realise there is more of Him to know.

This does not create dissatisfaction. It creates reverence, because the heart begins to understand that it is walking with One who is not only close but infinite in goodness, wisdom, and presence.

This is why eternity itself is described not as repetition but as ongoing life with God. "And this is eternal life, that they may know You, the only true God, and Jesus Christ whom You have sent" (John 17:3). Eternal life is defined relationally, knowing God, not as a completed event, but as an ongoing reality.

So, the invitation continues.

In prayer, in silence, in Scripture, in obedience, in ordinary moments of life, the believer is continually being drawn.

Sometimes gently.

Sometimes deeply.

Sometimes through joy.

Sometimes through conviction.

Sometimes through clarity.

Sometimes through mystery.

But always toward Him.

This is why the end of this book cannot be an end in the reader's heart. It is only a point of continuation. Intimacy with God is not concluded by reading about it. It is entered into by responding.

The final question, therefore, is not intellectual. It is relational.

Will you continue?

Will you remain open?

Will you keep drawing near?

Because the invitation has not ended.

It is still here.

It is still active.

It is still personal.

And it is still calling.

AFTERWORD

Some journeys begin with desire, and others begin with invitation. Intimacy with God is the latter. It is not the result of human ambition but the fruit of divine drawing. If you have reached this point, it is because God has been calling you closer, not into activity or performance, but into nearness.

The mystery of intimacy is that God does not ask the believer to climb towards Him; He calls the believer to yield. He does not demand perfection; He desires presence. He does not require eloquence; He invites honesty. He does not seek strength; He receives surrender.

This journey was never about reaching a destination but about awakening to the reality that God has always been near, and that intimacy is the life of those who learn to recognise Him.

Intimacy is not mastered; it is lived. It is not completed; it is deepened. It is not achieved; it is received.

The Holy Spirit will continue this work in you beyond these pages. He will teach you to dwell, to listen, to abide, to become still, and to live in awareness of God.

May your life become a secret place.
May your heart become an altar of awareness.
May your days become communion.
May your silence become fellowship.
May your nearness become union.

And may the God who called you into intimacy keep you in the reality of His presence all your days.

ACKNOWLEDGMENTS

Every book is a journey, but this one was a pilgrimage, a slow walk into the heart of God.

First, I acknowledge the Holy Spirit, the true Author of intimacy, the One who whispers, corrects, awakens, and sustains. Without Him, these pages are empty. With Him, they become an invitation to nearness.

I honour the spiritual voices, mentors, and vessels God has used to shape my walk with Him. Some spoke through teaching, others through silence, and others through example. Each contributed to the formation of a life that values presence over performance.

I acknowledge the community of believers who hunger for God, who refuse to settle for distance, who long for the secret place, and who are learning to recognise His voice again. Your hunger is not a weakness; it is evidence of life.

I honour every intercessor who has prayed unseen prayers, every quiet obedience that has carried others, and every hidden sacrifice made in love for God. Heaven remembers what people overlook.

And I acknowledge every reader of this book. May the same God who drew you to these pages draw you deeper into Himself.

ACKNOWLEDGMENT OF SPIRITUAL LINEAGE & GENERATIONAL CALL

Intimacy with God is never inherited through background, title, or position. It is inherited through hunger. Yet every generation stands on the shoulders of those who walked closely with God before them, choosing nearness over noise, obedience over recognition, and communion over performance.

I honour that spiritual lineage.

To the next generation:
Do not lose the wonder of God.
Do not trade His presence for productivity.
Do not mistake gifting for intimacy.
Do not let noise replace awareness.
Do not become too busy to be with Him.

You are called to be a generation that dwells, listens, lingers, recognises, and abides.

Your strength will not come from speed, but from nearness.
Your clarity will not come from noise, but from stillness.
Your authority will not come from performance, but from presence.

May you walk in intimacy with God in a way that reshapes your world.

NOTE ON ORIGIN & FORMATION OF THIS WORK

This book was not written from theory, research, or borrowed commentary. It was formed in prayer, shaped in stillness, and refined through communion with God.

Scripture remains the foundation of every truth expressed here, but the voice of this book is that of a lived encounter, the journey of learning nearness, awareness, and intimacy with God.

It is not a theological argument.
It is a spiritual witness.
It is not a manual of information.
It is an invitation into a relationship.

Every chapter reflects a movement of the heart from distance to awareness, from activity to communion, and from speaking about God to living with Him.

ABOUT THE AUTHOR

Oluwakemi T. Amuda writes from the hidden place, the quiet chambers where God shapes the soul in stillness and truth. Her life is anchored in the pursuit of God's presence, and her words carry the fragrance of one who has learned to linger before Him.

She is a student of the inner life, a watcher of the secret place, and a vessel committed to unveiling the mystery of intimacy with God.

Her calling is to guide believers into deeper awareness of God's presence, helping them move from spiritual activity to spiritual nearness, from distant awareness to an abiding relationship.

She does not write as an expert but as a witness, one who has tasted the nearness of God and cannot return to distance.

FINAL BENEDICTION

May the Lord bless you with a hunger that never fades.

May He continually draw you into awareness of His presence.

May He quiet your soul until His nearness becomes familiar.

May He awaken your spirit until His voice becomes recognisable.

May He lead you into the secret place and teach you to dwell there.

May intimacy become your atmosphere.

May prayer become your life.

May awareness of God become your identity.

And may the God who called you into nearness complete the work He has begun in you.

Amen.

www.ingramcontent.com/pod-product-compliance
Lightning Source LLC
LaVergne TN
LVHW090609110826
845146LV00001B/318
9798995645894